J. WARNER WALLACE

CASE CLOSED

A DETECTIVE INVESTIGATES THE RESURRECTION

CASE CLOSED
Published by David C Cook
4050 Lee Vance Drive
Colorado Springs, CO 80918 U.S.A.

Integrity Music Limited, a Division of David C Cook
Brighton, East Sussex BN1 2RE, England

ISBN 978-0-8307-9060-9
ISBN (10-pack) 978-0-8307-9061-6

Published in association with the literary agency of Mark Sweeney
& Associates, 302 Sherwood Drive, Carol Stream, IL 60188.
First edition titled *Alive*, ISBN 978-0-7814-1119-6. Portions of *Case Closed* are
taken from *Cold-Case Christianity: Updated and Expanded Edition*, published by
David C Cook, © 2013, 2023 J. Warner Wallace, ISBN 978-0-8307-8530-8.

The Team: Luke McKinnon, Jack Campbell, Susan Murdock
Cover Design: James Hershberger

Printed in India
Second Edition 2025

1 2 3 4 5 6 7 8 9 10

042825

Jesus *rose from the grave*. I knew this second claim about Jesus would change everything.

If Jesus truly rose from the tomb as the New Testament claims, He is more than just another smart guy. Buddha, Krishna, Confucius, Bahá'u'lláh, and Muhammad may have been smart, but they died just like everyone else. Jesus, according to the gospel authors, *defeated death altogether*. According to the Bible, Jesus isn't just a smart human; He's *God incarnate*. That puts Jesus in an entirely different category. I was willing to accept Jesus as a smart guy, but for me, the case related to His divine nature and resurrection was far from closed.

THINKING LIKE A DETECTIVE

Like most detectives, I'm innately skeptical. People lie, and I've learned to examine the evidence before adopting a claim. The pastor's assertion about the resurrection of Jesus was no different. But how could such a proposition about an ancient event be investigated evidentially? It's not as difficult as you might think, especially if you're willing to think *abductively.*

Abductive reasoning is also known as "inferring to the most reasonable explanation," and detectives employ this approach to examine crime scenes every day. Here's how it works: We enter a scene and start collecting and cataloging the raw facts (the evidence). Then we develop a list of possible explanations that might account for the evidence we've collected. Finally, we compare the evidence to the potential explanations and determine which explanation is, in fact, the most reasonable inference considering the evidential facts we've established.

The word *reasonable* is a critical aspect of abductive reasoning. If you're like me, you've probably learned the intuitive difference between what's possible and what's reasonable. When it comes right down to it, just about anything is possible. You may not even be reading this booklet right now, even though you think that you are. It's possible that aliens covertly kidnapped you last night and have induced a dreamlike, out-of-body, extraterrestrial hallucination. While you think this experience of reading is real, you may wake up tomorrow morning to discover yourself in an alien spaceship. But let's face it—that's not reasonable, is it?

It's interesting to imagine *possibilities*, but it's important to return eventually to what's *reasonable*, especially when the truth is at stake. That's why our criminal courts place a high standard on *reasonableness*, and that's important to remember as we think about the process of abductive reasoning. This rational approach to determining truth will help us come to the most reasonable conclusion in light of the evidence. It can be applied to more than criminal cases; we can apply the process of abduction to our spiritual investigations as well. But first, let's examine the concept with a real-life example from the world of homicide investigations.

ABDUCTIVE REASONING AND DEAD GUYS

Imagine we've been called out to a "dead-body scene"—a location where a deceased person has been discovered and the circumstances seem rather suspicious. While scenes like this are sometimes homicides, they are often less sinister; there are other possible explanations. Deaths fall into one of four categories: natural deaths, accidental deaths, suicides, or homicides. It's our job to figure out which of the four explanations is the most reasonable in the following scenario:

A young man was discovered on the floor of his apartment when his roommate returned from work. The man was lying facedown. The man was cold to the touch, nonresponsive, and stiff. Okay, given these minimal facts, it is clear that we actually do have a dead guy, but which of the four potential explanations is most reasonable given the facts? Is this death a natural death, an accident, a suicide, or a homicide?

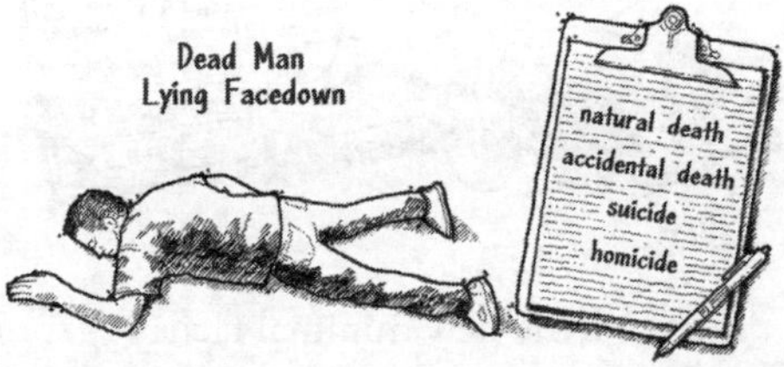

Given the minimal facts so far, all four of the potential explanations are still in play, aren't they? Unless we have something more to add evidentially, it will be difficult to decide if this case should be worked as a homicide or simply documented as something less criminal. Let's change the scenario slightly and add a new piece of evidence to see if it will help. Imagine that we entered the room and observed the man was lying in a pool of his own blood and this blood seemed to be coming from the area of his abdomen (under his body).

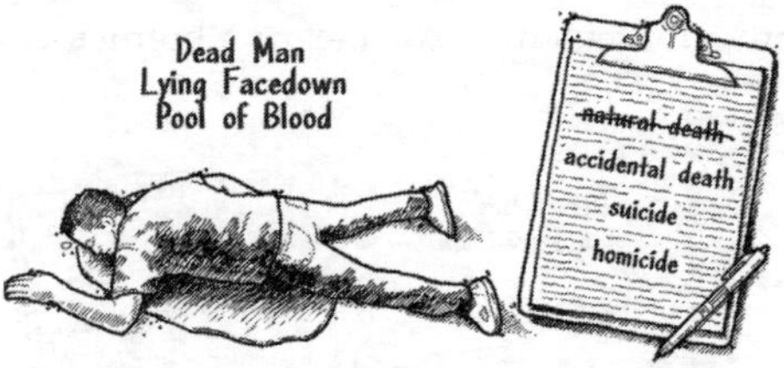

These are the new minimal facts: (1) A man is dead, (2) lying facedown on the floor, (3) in a pool of blood. Given this new set of facts, is there any direction our investigation might now take? Are any of our four explanations more (or less) reasonable than before?

Given the new evidence, we can reasonably remove the natural-death explanation from consideration. Since the man lacks a natural orifice from which to bleed in that part of his body, this inference seems unfounded; a natural death might be *possible*, but it isn't *reasonable*.

What about the other three explanations? Could this still be an accidental death? Sure, the man could have tripped and fallen on something (we wouldn't know until we turned him over). What about a suicide or a homicide? It seems these three remaining explanations are also still reasonable considering what limited evidence we have about this case. Until we learn a bit more, it will be difficult to decide which of these final three options is most reasonable.

Let's add a new dimension to the case. Imagine we enter the room and see the man lying on the floor in a pool of his own blood, but now we observe a large knife stuck in his lower back.

This presents us with a new set of facts: (1) The man is dead, (2) lying facedown on the floor, (3) in a pool of blood, and (4) there is a knife protruding from his lower back. The presence of a knife seems to eliminate the conclusion he died accidentally. An accidental death might be *possible* but it's not *reasonable*. If nothing else, the presence of the knife also confirms the unreasonable nature of a natural death. The most reasonable remaining explanations are either suicide or homicide, and suicide seems less and less likely, given the fact the victim's wound is located on his back. But since the wound is located in the *lower* portion of his back (within his reach), let's leave this option on the table for now.

Imagine, however, that a new fact has entered into our scenario. Imagine that we discover three extra wounds on the victim's upper back, in addition to the one we observed earlier.

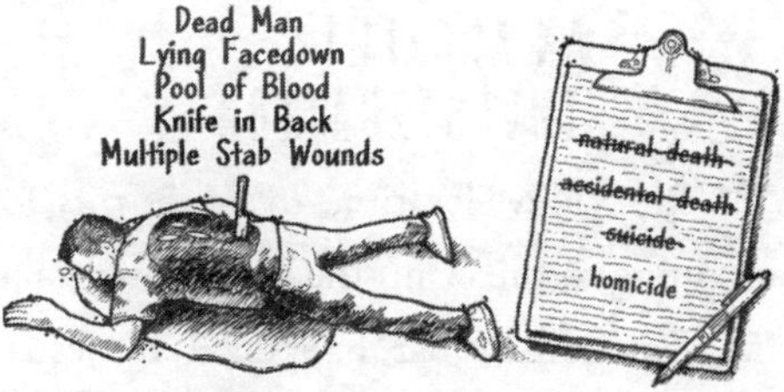

Our fact list now includes: (1) A man who is dead, (2) lying facedown on the floor, (3) in a pool of blood, (4) with multiple knife wounds on his back. Our reasonable explanations are dwindling, aren't they?

In this situation, natural death, accidental death, and suicide seem out of the question. While someone may argue they are still *possible*, few would recognize them as *reasonable*. The most reasonable conclusion considering the evidence is simply that this man was murdered. As responsible detectives, you and I would have no choice but to initiate a homicide investigation.

AN ANCIENT INVESTIGATION

Now it's time to apply this form of reasoning to the claim the pastor made about the resurrection. What happened to Jesus of Nazareth? How can we explain His empty tomb? Did His disciples steal His body? Was He only injured on the cross and later recovered? Did He actually die and resurrect from the dead?

I approached the investigation using the only tools I knew to use at the time: the tools of a detective. I began by making a list of facts and evidence. Next, I made a list of possible explanations for the evidence under consideration. Finally, I studied each explanation until I settled on the most reasonable inference from evidence.

Remember, I was a committed atheist at the time I started this endeavor. But even as an unbeliever, I was willing to grant a few essential factual claims related to Jesus:

1. Jesus died on the cross and was buried.
2. Jesus's tomb was empty, and no one ever produced His body.
3. Jesus's disciples believed that they saw Jesus resurrected from the dead.
4. Jesus's disciples were transformed following their alleged resurrection observations.

You'll notice none of these "minimal evidences" necessitate that Jesus truly rose from the grave. In my view as an atheist, any number of explanations could account for these facts. Let's look briefly at the potential explanations and list their associated difficulties (you can read *much* more about each explanation in *Cold-Case Christianity*).

THE DISCIPLES WERE WRONG ABOUT THE DEATH OF JESUS

Some skeptics think the disciples were mistaken about Jesus's death on the cross. They believe Jesus survived the beating and crucifixion and simply appeared to the disciples after He recovered.

THE PROBLEMS

This fails to satisfactorily explain what the disciples observed and experienced when they pulled Jesus from the cross. It's been my experience that witnesses who first come upon the dead body of someone they care about quickly check for the most obvious sign of life. Is the person who was injured *still breathing*? This test is simple and effective; everyone is capable of performing it, and even those who know nothing about human biology instinctively resort to it.

As a homicide detective, I've also observed three conditions common to the bodies of dead people (known as the "Mortis Triad"). Dead people lose warmth until they eventually reach the temperature of their environment. They begin to feel "cold to the touch" (this is known as *algor mortis*). In addition, chemical reactions begin to take place in the muscles after death occurs, resulting in stiffening and rigidity known as *rigor mortis*. Dead people become rigid, retaining the shape they were in when they died. Finally, when the heart stops beating, blood begins to pool in the body, responding to the force of gravity (a condition known as *livor mortis*). As a result, purple discoloration becomes apparent in those areas of the body that are closest to the ground. In essence, dead bodies look, feel, and respond differently than living, breathing humans do. Is it reasonable to believe that those who removed Jesus from the cross, took possession of His body, carried Him to the grave, and spent time treating and wrapping His body for burial would not have noticed any of these conditions common to dead bodies?

In addition to this, the Gospels record the guard stabbed Jesus and observed both blood and water pouring from His body. That's an important observation, given that the gospel writers were not coroners or medical doctors. I've been to my share of coroners' autopsies, and I've spoken at length with coroner investigators at crime scenes. When people are injured to the point of death, they often enter into some form of "circulatory shock" prior to dying (due to the fact that their organs and body tissues are not receiving adequate blood flow). This can sometimes result in either "pericardial effusion" (increased fluid in the membrane surrounding the heart) or "pleural effusion" (increased fluid in the membrane surrounding the lungs). When Jesus was pinned to the cross in an upright position following the terrible flogging He received, it's reasonable to expect this kind of effusion might have taken place in response to circulatory shock. These fluids would certainly pour out of His body if He were pierced with a spear. While the gospel writers might expect to see blood, their surprising observation of the water is certainly consistent with the fact Jesus was already dead when stabbed by the guard.

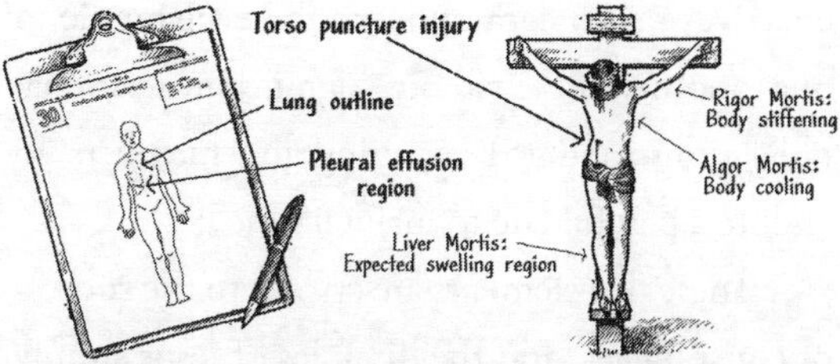

THE DISCIPLES LIED ABOUT THE RESURRECTION

Some non-Christians claim the disciples stole the body from the grave and then fabricated the stories of Jesus's resurrection appearances.

THE PROBLEMS

This explanation fails to account for the transformed lives of the apostles. In my years working robberies, I had the opportunity to investigate (and break) a number of conspiracy efforts, and I learned about the nature of successful conspiracies. As a result, I'm skeptical of conspiracy theories requiring the joint effort of (1) many people, (2) over a significant period of time, (3) with no effective way to communicate the evolving lie to one another, (4) without significant relational obligations, and (5) requiring the members to endure a painful fate to maintain the lie.

These five elements are critical to the success of conspiracies, and the disciples of Jesus simply lacked what it would take to be successful. There were too many witnesses (over five hundred according to the New Testament), holding the "lie" for too long (over six decades), without any way to communicate and facing tortuous consequences. Add to this the fact they lacked any motive for such a lie. This explanation for the resurrection is simply unreasonable.

3 THE DISCIPLES WERE DELUSIONAL

Some skeptics believe the disciples, as a result of their intense grief and sorrow, only *imagined* seeing Jesus alive after His death on the cross. These critics claim the appearances were simply hallucinations resulting from wishful thinking.

THE PROBLEMS

This explanation fails to account for the diversity of the resurrection observations. Whenever I suspect someone may have imagined (or simply misinterpreted) an observation, I rely on a *cumulative* approach to establish the truth. Are there additional accounts I can compare to corroborate the statement? What is the most reasonable inference based on *all* available sources? The resurrection accounts, for example, are diverse and robust.

Jesus appeared to groups of varying sizes, at a variety of locations and times, involving both friends and strangers, for differing purposes and varying periods of time, as recorded by multiple authors. It's unlikely these diverse observations are all simply hallucinations. While *individuals* have hallucinations, there are no examples of large *groups* of people having the exact same hallucination. Even if a short, momentary group hallucination could seem reasonable, long, sustained, and detailed hallucinations are unsupported historically and intuitively unreasonable.

THE DISCIPLES WERE FOOLED BY AN IMPOSTER

Some skeptics believe an imposter tricked the disciples and convinced them Jesus was still alive; the disciples then unknowingly advanced the lie.

THE PROBLEMS

Many of my partners spent several years investigating fraud and forgery crimes prior to joining us on the homicide team. I've learned a lot from these investigators, including what it takes to pull off a successful con. Accomplished con artists must (1) win the *confidence* of those they are trying to fool (hence the title "con" artist), and (2) know more about the subject of the deception than the person being deceived. The less the victim understands about the specific topic and area in which they are being "conned," the more likely the con artist will be successful. Victims are often fooled and swindled out of their money because they have little or no expertise in the area in which the con artist is operating. The perpetrator can use sophisticated language and make claims outside the victim's expertise. The crook *sounds* legitimate, primarily because the victim doesn't really know what truly *is* legitimate.

When the targeted victim knows more about the subject than the person attempting the con, the odds are good the perpetrator will fail at his attempt to fool the victim. For this reason, the proposal that a sophisticated first-century con artist fooled the disciples seems unreasonable.

Charles Ponzi
A Famous Con Artist

An Alleged Imposter
An Unreasonable Con Artist

5 THE DISCIPLES WERE INFLUENCED BY LIMITED SPIRITUAL SIGHTINGS

Some atheists believe one or two of the disciples had a vision of the risen Christ and then convinced the others these spiritual sightings were legitimate. They believe additional sightings simply came as a response to the intense influence of the first visions.

THE PROBLEMS

This fails to explain the empty tomb and explains the resurrection observations in a manner inconsistent with the biblical record. It's not unusual to have a persuasive witness influence the beliefs of other eyewitnesses. I've investigated a number of murders in which one emphatic witness has persuaded others that something occurred, even though the other witnesses weren't even present to see the event for themselves. But these *persuaded witnesses* were easily distinguished from the one who *persuaded them* once I began to ask for *their* account of what happened. Only the persuader possessed the details in their most robust form. For this reason, his or her account was typically the most comprehensive, while the others tended to generalize since they didn't actually see the event for themselves. In addition, when pressed to repeat the story of the one persuasive witness, the other witnesses eventually pointed to that witness as their source. While it's possible for a persuasive witness to convince some of the other witnesses his or her version of events is the true story, I've never encountered a persuader who could convince *everyone*. The more witnesses who are involved in a crime, the less likely all of them will be influenced by any one eyewitness, regardless of that witness's charisma or position within the group.

This theory also suffers from all the liabilities of the earlier claim the disciples *imagined* the resurrected Christ. Even if the persuader could convince everyone of his or her first observation, the subsequent *group visions* are still unreasonable for all the reasons we've already discussed.

6 THE DISCIPLES' OBSERVATIONS WERE DISTORTED LATER

Some unbelievers claim the original observations of the disciples were amplified and distorted as the legend of Jesus grew over time. These skeptics believe Jesus may have been a wise teacher but argue the resurrection is a legendary and historically late exaggeration.

THE PROBLEMS

This explanation fails to explain the early claims of the apostles related to the resurrection. Cold-case detectives investigate the possibility of "legendary" distortions and evidential alterations more than other types of detectives. Given the passage of time, it's important to make sure stories haven't changed and evidence hasn't been altered. How do we accomplish this task of verification? By tracing the "chain of custody."

Did the witness tell people about his or her observations over the years? Did the people who heard the statements document what they heard? If there is an important piece of physical evidence (say, for example, a *button* found in the crime scene), did the original detectives photograph and document its condition over the years as it was transported to and from the property room or the crime lab? We can compare the statements, reports, and photographs related to these witnesses and evidence to trace any potential changes over time. Each report acts as a link in the "chain" connecting the descriptions of the past to the evidence presented today.

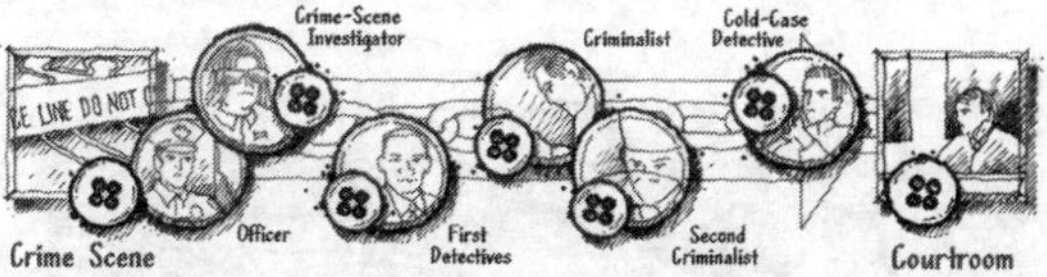

The "chain of custody" for the claims related to the resurrection is robust. In the earliest accounts of the disciples' activity after the crucifixion, they cite the resurrection of Jesus as their primary piece of evidence that Jesus was God. From the earliest days of the Christian movement, eyewitnesses were making this claim. The next links in the historic "chain of custody" confirm the story of the resurrection remained unchanged. The students of the disciples *also* recorded the resurrection was a key component of the disciples' eyewitness testimony. In fact, the earliest-known Christian creed or oral record (as described by Paul in 1 Corinthians 15) includes the resurrection as a key component. The claim of the resurrection occurs early in Christian history, and it doesn't change over the years.

7 THE DISCIPLES ACCURATELY REPORTED THE RESURRECTION

Christians, of course, claim Jesus truly rose from the dead. They believe the Gospels contain accurate eyewitness accounts of this event.

THE PROBLEMS

It would be naive, however, to accept this explanation without recognizing a *liability* highlighted by skeptics and nonbelievers. The claim

Jesus truly rose from the dead presents the following concern and objection: the explanation requires a belief in the supernatural: a belief that Jesus had the supernatural power to rise from the dead in the first place.

ABDUCTIVE REASONING AND THE RESURRECTION

I limited the evidence to four modest claims about the resurrection and kept my explanatory options open to all the possibilities (both *natural* and *supernatural*). The last explanation (although it is a miraculous, supernatural explanation) suffers from the least number of liabilities and deficiencies, while retaining the greatest explanatory power.

Allow me to illustrate it a different way. When it comes down to the claims about the resurrection, there are just two possibilities: Jesus either (A) rose from the dead or (B) He didn't. It's really that simple.

As a committed philosophical naturalist who rejected supernatural explanations, I was inclined to select *option B*. But all the naturalistic theories typically offered to explain the evidence related to Jesus were simply insufficient. Each stood as an obstacle, preventing me from reasonably reaching the conclusion the resurrection was untrue.

The Christian explanation for the resurrection involved a far less encumbered path. It only required me to jump one hurdle: my presuppositional bias against the supernatural. If I was willing to enter the investigation without this preexisting bias, the Christian explanation accounted for the evidence most simply and most exhaustively. It is logically consistent (if we simply allow for the existence of God in the first place). It is also superior to the other accounts (given it does not suffer from all the problems we see with the other explanations).

If we approach the issue of the resurrection in an unbiased manner (without the presuppositions described in the previous section) and assess it as we evaluated the dead-body scene, we can judge the possible explanations and eliminate those that are unreasonable. The conclusion that Jesus was resurrected (as reported in the Gospels) can be sensibly inferred from the available evidence. The resurrection *is reasonable*.

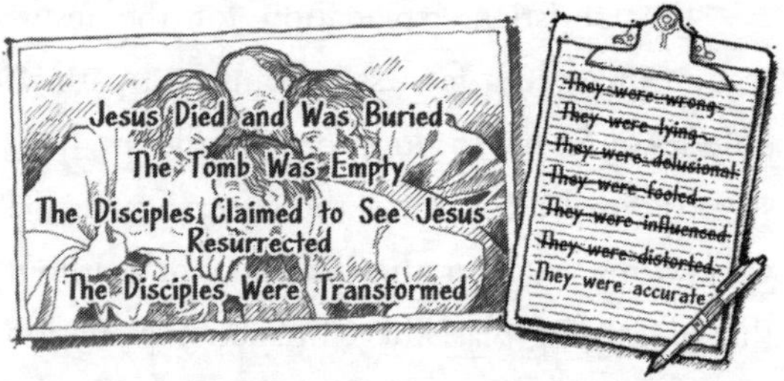

MOVING FROM THE MOST REASONABLE INFERENCE TO A DECISION TO TRUST

It's one thing to believe *that* Jesus rose from the dead and is who He said He was, but it's another to believe *in* Him as Savior. Every one of us, at some point in our investigation of the claims of Christianity, has to move from "belief that" to "belief in." I can remember when this happened for me. As a rebellious, self-reliant detective, I initially denied my *need* for a Savior, even though I accepted what the Gospels told me *about* that Savior. In order to take a step from "belief that" to "belief in," I needed to move from an examination of *Jesus* to an examination of *me*. As I read the Gospels for a second (and third) time and explored all of the New Testament Scripture, I began to focus more on what it said about *me* than what it said about *Jesus*. I didn't like what I saw.

Even though I was a law enforcement officer, I knew "bad guys" weren't the only ones who messed up. *Everyone* violates moral laws at one time or another, and I was no exception. The ancient authors of the Bible also understood "all have sinned and fall short of the glory of God" (Romans 3:23). If there is an all-powerful Creator, He is the one morally perfect Being. He is, in fact, categorically different than fallen human beings.

I also knew there was a *consequence* for crime. A God who cares about justice would surely enforce the law, and the Bible declares the penalty our sin deserves: "the wages of sin is death" (Romans 6:23). As imperfect beings, we simply cannot be united to a morally perfect God unless we somehow pay the penalty for sin. To remain in our sin is to be eternally separated from a sinless God. This, in and of itself, is bad news for *all* of us.

Unless, of course, there is a remedy.

God, in His *grace*, provides a way to satisfy His *justice*: "The gracious gift of God is eternal life in Christ Jesus our Lord" (Romans 6:23). God offers us eternal life even though we don't deserve it. He paid the price for our sins *Himself*, and He had us in His sights, even when we weren't looking for Him: "God demonstrates His own love toward us, in that while we were still sinners, Christ died for us" (Romans 5:8).

The gospel of Jesus Christ is good news. God offers imperfect humans—even an imperfect police officer like me—a perfect eternity. No strings attached. It's a gift. We simply have to accept it. "If you confess with your mouth Jesus as Lord, and believe in your heart that God raised Him from the dead, you will be saved" (Romans 10:9).

I can still remember the day this clicked for me. I was working on an open, unsolved case as an undercover detective, sitting in an unmarked surveillance car, waiting for a suspect to leave his house. I was parked next to a schoolyard on the perimeter of the surveillance, reading the letters of Paul. I was slowly moving from "belief that" to "belief in," shifting from belief that Jesus is who He said He was (God incarnate who came to take the punishment we deserve) to a surrendered acceptance of His sacrifice on the cross (where He paid the penalty for my sin). That's when I knew it was time to put my trust in Jesus, confident that "everyone who calls on the name of the Lord will be saved" (Romans 10:13).

After spending months investigating the gospel accounts, I was now certain. Unlike the open, unsolved case I was investigating as part of our agency's surveillance team, the case for the resurrection was *closed*. Jesus died on a cross and rose from the grave. The evidence is sufficient. The conclusion is reasonable. If you're interested in wisdom like I was when I started this journey, Jesus is worth the investigation. Unlike other wise, ancient sages, Jesus offers wisdom and *peace with God*. Let the good news change your life. "Therefore, having been justified by faith, we have peace with God through our Lord Jesus Christ" (Romans 5:1). "There is now no condemnation at all for those who are in Christ Jesus" (Romans 8:1), because "neither death, nor life, nor angels, nor principalities, nor things present, nor things to come, nor powers, nor height, nor depth, nor any other created thing will be able to separate us from the love of God that is in Christ Jesus our Lord" (Romans 8:38–39).